The Return of Cupid

Outdated 90's romance

UK Edition

The Return of Cupid
Outdated 90's romance

UK Edition

Copyrights @UKinkers 2022

The following is a work of fiction. Any names, characters, places and incidents are the product of the author's imagination. Any resemblance to persons, living or dead, is entirely coincidental.

ISBN   978-1-7392970-0-8

All rights reserved. No part of this publication may be reproduced, scanned, or transmitted in any form, digital or printed, without the written permission of the author.

Cover Design & book Formatting: UKinkers

www.sherifelhotabiy.com

www.ukinkers.com

Dedication

To

Dame Dominique
Natalie - counting stars together
Dr. Hala Banna
Dr. Youssreya Abou-Hadid

&

My Mother

About the Author

Born in 1978 in London –the UK, then moved to Cairo, Egypt, in the early 1980s.

He started writing poetry in school, and during college, he won first prize in the English poetry contest for three consecutive years.

Also, during college, he became co-head of the poetry club in Egypt's best-selling English magazine.

After graduating in computer & management sciences, he joined Nile TV international as an editor, then moved up to be an editor-in-chief, reporter and news anchor.

He later used his creative and writing skills in public relations, advertisement, marketing, and copyrighting.

After spending six years writing his first novel, he sent the manuscript to Her Majesty the Queen to reward himself morally.

After successfully publishing his novel in Egypt, he founded UKinkers.com to publish 'The Merchant' in the UK.

Join UK inkers

We aim to gather all the people required for a successful publisher in one meeting point. Of course, we start with the writers and connect them with publishers, editors, agents, bookstores, book designers, filmmakers, PR & marketing experts, and even logistical and payment solution providers.

How does it work?

Authors send us their work. Then we feature authors we find offering an addition to the literary scene. Interested publishers and agents approach them, and authors contact editors, book designers or whomever they need to get their books to the scene.

And then, it all begins, and we add authors to the scene and enrich the literature further.

Whom are we starting with?

Extraordinary authors and whoever is ready to step out of the mainstream and join our community that works for the benefit of the Word, whether written in ink or pixels.

Why focus on the UK?

It is the capital of literature—the 'Hollywood' of books and the royal court of authors.

www.ukinkers.com

Intro

Unlike today, romantic love was a big deal to teenagers in the 90s. The songs we listened to were romantic and charged with passionate emotions. The Films we watched were all about finding the one and only true love. I was one of those teenagers, fed every day with the hunger of finding true love. In & out of relationships, failed attempts and heartbreaks at that age made me see the cycle. The cycle of realizing & admiring beauty, falling in love with it, and in case the relationship doesn't work, heartbreaks. The agony that pushes one to find wisdom and then finally find one's own self. I perceived this cycle as the five senses of the soul.

If you want to take a raw, unedited & insightful into a 90s romantic teenager's perception of love, take a dive into passionate emotions and read this book.

Sherif,

UKinkers.com

The Return of Cupid

v

The Return of Cupid

Outdated 90's romance

UK Edition

Copyrights @UKinkers 2022

The following is a work of fiction. Any names, characters, places and incidents are the product of the author's imagination. Any resemblance to persons, living or dead, is entirely coincidental.

ISBN   978-1-7392970-0-8

All rights reserved. No part of this publication may be reproduced, scanned, or transmitted in any form, digital or printed, without the written permission of the author.

Cover Design & book Formatting: UKinkers

www.sherifelhotabiy.com

www.ukinkers.com

Prologue

Beauty is the first chapter of this book, because it is the first & basic feeling of love. We see beauty first then we fall in love with it.
But unfortunately love can't always survive the storm.
Which leaves us at the end with a broken heart.
A broken heart leaves us no choice, we got to grow wise in order to go on.
And only then we discover who we really are.
And only then we can fall in love again, only then Cupid can return to our skies.

First Sense

When Cupid opened his eyes he saw the most beautiful girl in the world walking on the opposite pavement. He fell deeply in love with her. He could hear or see no one but her. He stood up in front of her but he couldn't utter a word as her eyes shocked him with their beauty.

Beauty

The Soprano

With no jet or plane,
Your eyes took me to Spain,
With no car or train,
Your smile took me to France,
Leaving behind agony and pain,
For a fresh blend of romance,
Without leaving the house,
Or even my room,
Your singing voice,
Took me to Rome,
Without passing a door or a gate,
You served me Mexico on a plate,
And lit me the candles of India,
On an Arabian night,
Bringing me the stars of china,
In the middle of the west,
You are my prize, my medallion, my academy award,
For I have given you my heart ... and in return ... you gave me ... the world.

The Fairy
(To Liv Taylor in the Lord of the Rings: The Two Towers)

What beauty on Earth could that be?
What heavenly face do I see?
What skies
have you been through,
That gave such eyes
So blue,
What milky river have you bathed in,
That gave you such fair white skin,
What kind of fruits,
What kind of grape,
That gave you such lips,
So fine in shape,
What music have you heard,
That gave the voice of a hummingbird,
Which sun have you embraced,
To give you such warmth that never fades,
Which star have been created when you were born,
For it will be the place that I'll always look upon.

You Give Love
(To women)

> You give love a sound when you talk,
> You give love life when you walk,
> You give love style,
> When you smile,
> You give love flavour,
> With your feminine behaviour,
> You give love meaning,
> When I watch you breathing,
> You give love a view,
> When I look at you,
> So don't you understand,
> That when I kiss your hand,
> Is the least I can do,
> When I see love … through you.

A Glance
(To Reem)

I saw a land with rivers and streams,
A green land that could only be seen in dreams,
I saw a star moving swiftly going up and down,
I saw a mountain queen with a rainbow crown,
I saw innocence in its natural form,
I knew where beauty comes from,
I saw the sun teaching a young moon how to set and rise,
Then when you touched my hand I came to realize that I was just looking into your eyes.

At Your Beauty
(To Mai)

So much beauty in you I can see,
My dream girl is what you mean to me,
So much beauty, in your eyes, in your lips,
I wonder how beautiful would be your kiss,
So much smooth, smooth is your brown skin,
I can feel it just like a breeze from Heaven,
Your eye, your hair, reminds me of a Romantic night,
They are dark, they are black but so attractive and bright,
It could never be human beauty,
It's too good to be true,
I've seen a fairy, but maybe I did when I saw you,
Hide your beauty, by Heaven's sake,
Thousands of hearts are what it may break,
At your beauty, I can never ... not stare,
But, loving you, my heart won't dare.

Second Sense

As Cupid entered a restaurant after the girl, he didn't know what to do. He was running out of time as he sat on his chair and watched his beloved at a distant table.

Suddenly and without any hesitation, he approached her and said:

"I know that I've annoyed you all day long but I have never seen such a beauty before. Your beauty is so difficult to resist and so easy to hang on to, I am not asking you to fall in love with me because I know that Cupid is out of bows because his last golden bow was hit in my heart for me to love you.

If he was merciless to my heart please don't be the same.... A dance all I am asking you is one dance, one dance for my heart to feel a bit of warmth that would help it to carry on.

He took her hand and they started to dance on the dance floor. Both of them couldn't recognize what kind of dance, tango, waltz...Whatever. All they knew was that it was a dance of love.

Love

Confession

I can't fly but I can see the flying birds,
I can't sing but I can hear their songs,
I can't swim but I can catch fish,
I am not a prince but I can make a wish,
I can't bring you the stars,
But I can point out Mars,
I can't see the air but I can feel it blow,
I can't stop the river but I can watch it flow,
I can't kill hate but I can let it go,
I don't own fire but I can warm you in snow,
Isn't that enough for you to accept my love?
Isn't that enough for you to respect my life,
To respect the way I feel,
To take my dreams for real,
This is how I see myself as truly as ever,
I don't know how you see me but whatever,
You must know that I will never,
Love you less than forever.

I Wish

I want to hold you, I want to kiss you; yes I do,
Does that make me in love with you?,
I want to pass my fingers through your hair,
While lulling you on a rocking chair,
I want to feel your breath, watch you laugh,
I want to get you everything you wished to have,
Does that make me in love with you?,
And again I want to lay a kiss,
On your forehead, your palm, and you finger-tips,
Oh I swear I want to,
Does that make me in love with you?,
God help me if I do,
As long as its not me that you belong to.

I.L.U

She asked me about love,
What shall I tell her?
It's as sweet as a dove,
As Heavenly as thunder,
It's a Holy gift from God to us,
Yes, maybe that is what it is,
It's passion, fantasy, glory and pain,
It's a river a storm, it's the wind and the rain,
Many things are said about love
Could be false
Could be true,
Many things that I don't care about
Because to me
Love is you.

Nature

Ask me why, where, how, or what,
Ask me whatever you want ... I will answer not,
Ask and ask, and listen to yourself while asking,
Listen and try to look at yourself from where I'm standing,
Ask yourself...why do the stars come out at night,
Ask yourself ... why does the sun give the moon its light,
Why do children fly a kite,
And why do we see colorus ... blue, green, and white,
Why does the breeze,
Move the leaves,
Why do the sunset shed the sky with a rosy hue,
Why do the trees sprinkle each morning with due,
Answer me, I don't think you can ever do,
Because if so, you would have never asked me,
Why am I in love with you?

Third Sense

At the end of the dance, Cupid's wings started to open and they were completely healed.

In a second Cupid left her and ran away as he reached a small empty area behind the restaurant, his wings opened and spread in the air, they were back as strong and beautiful as ever.

And that only meant one thing that Cupid has to return, and leave his beloved behind.

For now he will not just leave her behind, but he will also have to strike her heart one day, and make her fall in love, with another.

Cupid fell on his knees, crying, and suffering from a broken heart.

Heart Breaks

Under the Christmas Tree

Sitting watching the Christmas tree,
Lonely wishing you next to me,
Watching the lights
Off and on,
Kept watching all night
Till dawn,
Watching the snow all over the tree,
Wishing your beauty instead to see,
Hearing the music passing through my ears,
As the candles slowly dropped their waxy tears,
A tear after a tear,
Reminding me that you are not here,
Through all the sadness, you are still my dear,
And I can't stop myself,
From sending you love,
And wishing you a happy New Year.

Alternatives

Been to the fruits market,
Checking each pile and basket,
Mangos, cherries, apples,
Different scents and colorus,
I tasted each and drank its juice,
But non-seemed to resemble the taste of yours,
So I turned to another shop,
At which I made another stop,
Checked all the silk,
Pink and blue,
Still, nothing felt as smooth as you,
Went to the jeweller
Brought the latest, the classic,
And the bizarre,
Pearls and diamonds
Didn't seem as precious as you are,
Went to the music store,
But couldn't make a choice,
I listened and listened more,
But nothing sounds like your voice,
At the end of the day,
To home, I made my way,
With a hand holding an empty bag,
And a heart crying for his beloved ... to come back.

Rainy Sky of Love

Walking in the streets of the Old Town,
Old ornaments, classical music, and a gramophone,
Old pictures of Cupid and a crying clown,
Watching them as I've been walking all alone,
In that place which they called "The Lovers' Zone".
Then there was that old man, riding a carriage loaded with old stuff,
On which I saw the picture of the prettiest girl I've ever seen in my life,
Suddenly, and I don't know why I started following it,
The same picture of the girl whom I always wanted to get.
Madly I found myself running even the people I started to push,
I want to reach that picture, now that's all that I wish,
As it seemed close I felt happy as a bird flying in the sky,
But the place was crowded, and I lost it as it did turn its way,
And now,
Everybody is running as the sky did heavily rain,
And now,
I am standing, as I was lonely again,
Helplessly,
I dropped to my knees, staring at the path of the old shops,
Slowly,
As I heard, there was a sound of footsteps;

The Return of Cupid

It's the old man, without the carriage, as I saw him I did cry,
He laid his hand over my shoulder and whispered:
"Son, Birds don't own their Sky".

A Dreamy Dawn

One star, Two stars, and three,
Face to face, as if staring at me,
Hours by hours with no single word,
But what they want to say I've already heard,
Stop blaming me, just let me sink in my sadness,
Fires are burning,
Yes, I do miss that kind of madness,
Where is my love?
Could be with you or with the other,
Or maybe I won't have
That love I may find never,
I'm searching for my love
In every face
And every place, too,
But maybe my love
Doesn't need me
as much as
I do,
I can't forget about it,
I can't kill my hope,
I can't stab my heart,
I can't let it beats stop.
I am staring at the sky

At the stars, and at the moon,
Dreaming of my love
Over that cold grass, I am laying on,
So let me sink into my dreams
Over that green hill,
Ask me no questions
And have no words to tell,
But if you really want to help me
And want my fires to rest,
Bring me a Rose, from my love,
And drop its dew ... over my chest.

Doctor Love

The doctor prescribed me love to cure,
But it is not sold in any pharmacy or store,
In lies in the hearts of a sweetie cutie female,
And those who try to reach it usually fail,
A yes means a no,
And a no means a yes,
It has nothing to do with you,
But this is the way it is,
Try and fail think and guess,
Decorate your cheek with a goodbye kiss,
Follow her from china to Vancouver,
One step wrong and the game is over,
No doctor I don't think so and let me make it clear,
If you haven't noticed my broken heart…LOVE…is what
Got me here.

Fourth Sense

Soon the angels appeared in front of him to welcome him back.

"Why do I have to leave now? Why do I have to leave my beloved just as I am getting closer to her?" Cupid cried. "I won't go, I am staying here," he said nervously.

"But if you stay you'll die and Cupid won't exist anymore," an angel said.

"It doesn't matter, I can't leave my love," Cupid replied.

"And what about their love? What about their emotions? Do you want to sacrifice it all for her sake? Did you forget, Cupid who you are, the angel of love, she is not yours. You are not her love. If you stay you will destroy everything even her.

Tomorrow is valentine's day and a lot of people are waiting for you. Come on Cupid, come on....". Cupid laid his head on the angel's shoulder holding him strongly and crying madly.

Once again the two angels flew up together, high in the sky and Cupid returned to the

Clouds and the mountain peaks, with a broken heart

And in a way a wiser mind.

Wisdom

Windy Life

Once upon a winter breeze,
Passing smoothly through the trees,
Moving the branches and lulling the leaves,
A young lady dropped to her knees,
Watering the woods with her tears,
Did you feel it?
Or did it feel you?
Whether it is a yes or a no,
It can't stay around draining your pain,
Whatever comes must surely go,
And you just have to wait again.

Poverty

Do you always walk with your feet bear,
On this winter cold floor?
About you, no one bothered to care just because you are **poor**,
Do you always play with stones and sand,
Had anybody ever put a candy in your hand?
A little sweet girl with her hair cruelly shaved,
She almost broke my heart when she smiled at me and **waved**,
Maybe still there is a lot she is hopeful for,
Maybe she is still cheerful waiting for Santa to knock on her door.

When a Sailor Speaks

I've been a sailor for over a million sunrise,
I travelled the seven seas. I saw millions of tides,
I saw the legendary sea monsters,
There ... up there ... where there is no rule but the captain's,
Is that really the way it is?
No rule but the captain's?
But what would the captain do if the powerful sea un-caged his anger,
What would the captain do if his sight is blinded by thunder?
Nothing.
Nothing can I say than I love the sea,
I feel everything out there is in love with me,
The whales ... the cups ... and my faithful bottle of wine,
That cries each time when it will no longer be mine,
Or maybe these are happy tears because I'll be drunk no more,
Because at last, I'd find my way back to the shore,
There's only the sky and the sea but I've learnt a lot,
More than you've ever thought,
In the sea, it doesn't matter if the sun rises at dusk or at dawn,
What matter is that it never rises alone.

A little Girl's Wish

A little girl stepped slowly,
Towards the wishing well,
She touched it gently,
With so much to tell,
After she whispered,
I saw on her face that big smile,
And everything was so silent for a while,
Suddenly, so many Birds came out to fly,
So many, until they reached the sky,
That little girl made a wish,
she made it right,
We all needed to see such a cloud,
not grey, but white.

A Woman ... A Rose

I grabbed my chair to stand,
And walked directly towards your table,
Unless this Rose in my hand,
Walking, I wouldn't be able,
Would you take this Rose from me but it is not just a Rose,
It`s a symbol of love as everybody knows,
But why do lovers choose a red coloured Rose to be for love a symbol?
It is hard to tell though the answer is simple,
Have you ever seen a woman...I mean her inner self...her soul?
Could be young, dry, and wild but still beautiful after all,
Have you ever seen a lady without a scent?
Her perfume is not what I meant,
No man can touch with his lips a lady's skin,
Without noticing her beauty within,
A Rose is a huge piece of beauty but it can never be left without somebody's care,
Maybe the sun, the bees, the breeze, or just a man, that to her beauty does stare,
Lovers choose a lot to symbolise love but what I know,
Where ever there is beauty, there are you.

Fifth Sense

He had to shed romance again upon the entire world. So Cupid struck the earth, striking every human he saw.

Romantic songs, red roses, chocolates, love cards were back again. It was the best valentine's humans had ever lived. Everybody on earth was in love as Cupid struck all his bows in their hearts.

And as all humans celebrated this very special occasion, and the air filled with more and more romance, Cupid was left in sad romantic mood forever.

He flew far away and he
Stayed on a mountaintop writing poems and making new love bows.

The Return of Cupid

The Poet

Moments

Sometimes I ask myself,
When was the most beautiful moment of my life,
Was it ... when I fell in love at first sight?
Or when I was walking a girl home at night?
Was it ... when rain socked us wet?
Or when I first felt your scent?
Was it ... when we were riding horses like a prince and a princess,
Or when we're swiftly dancing on ice?
Was it ... when I got you chocolates to make you taste how sweet you are,
Was it ... when we were laying and waiting for a shooting star?
Was it when I first saw you?
I don't know,
Whatever was the most beautiful moment of my life there was I and you ... and a little bit of Love.

Me 2

She asked me who am I,
And what do I do?
I smiles and answered her… 'me' is all in 2,
I have two names… two homes, and I'm a Gemini,
I think twice and when I lose I give myself a second try,
I have two houses, two jobs, and two flags,
Two talents and two favourite songs,
Two looks, two perfumes and two smiles,
Elegant and wild…are my two different lifestyles,
And I'll say it again me is all in two,
And I can love you as twice as anyone can do.

Flying Heart

In love … I've always been,
Never thought I won't desire love again,
To be in love you must fall in love,
And I no longer want to fall,
A broken heart scratches deep into the soul,
I will no longer be held back by roses and cards,
With freedom, I will cross millions of yards,
It's time for elevation,
Time for a new start,
I'll rule my own fair nation,
And oust my tyrant heart,
It is no longer time for any fools,
From now on the game runs with my own rules,
Once I heard an African man say,
"No woman … No cry",
And as of today,
It's time for my heart to fly.

Explaination

You tempt me with your glances,
It's hard for a man to resist your smiles,
But between us, there is a distance,
A huge gap of a million miles,
You are not my beloved and you've never been,
I am not a sinner and your love for me is a sin,
You are beautiful but your beauty doesn't satisfy my needs,
Your beauty is a garden but I've never thrown its seeds,
Your breath swims through the air without my scent,
Your friends are people I've never met,
Your eyes are stars that don't belong to my sky,
Your joy is a sunrise but not upon my day,
You are not my beloved so I have to go back,
Sorry, but I can't step on land that doesn't hold my flag.

Brightness
(To my muse)

        I've never met the queen of diamonds,
           She gave me one though,
           One diamond in my hand
           One long way to go,
Start your journey in romance, words, and meanings,
           Your heart is your guide
           Your fortune is feelings,
           This diamond is your lamp,
           The Human heart is your map,
           If you are faithful enough,
           In humans' love,
      You will feel their pain as if its is yours,
      So cure their hearts, minds, and souls,
It is not an easy thing to do, but this is your duty,
      Fade pain, find joy, and spread beauty.

"Personal Quote"

"Art is made of the droplets of the steam of our feelings after it hits the cold surface of reality"

Sherif El Hotabiy

The 90s greatest romances

A glimpse of some films & songs that made every teenager a hopeless romantic

Films:

- Sleepless in Seattle
- It could happen to you
- When Harry met Sally
- Notting Hill
- Forrest Gump
- Only you
- Jerry Maguier
- Reality Bites
- Edward Scissorhands
- Top gun
- Brave Heart
- Don Juan DeMarco
- The Body Gurad
- The Blue Lagoon
- A Walk to remember
- She is all that
- The Mask of Zorro
- Titanic
- One Fine Day
- Nine Months

- City of Angels
- Pretty Woman
- Sense and Sensibility
- Ten Thing I Hate About You
- Fools Rush In
- You've Got Mail
- While you were Sleeping
- How to lose a guy in 10 days
- Grosse Pointe Blank
- A Walk in the Clouds
- Far and Away

Songs:

- Lady in Red
- No Ordinary Love
- Kiss me
- Un-Break My Heart
- 2 Become 1
- Hero
- Kiss from a rose
- You are still the one
- From this moment on
- I'll make love to you
- Baby, I love your way
- Back for Good
- How deep is your love
- My Heart will go on
- Without you
- Love is all around
- I don't want to miss a thing
- Always
- When a man loves a woman
- My All
- I swear
- Truly Madly Deeply
- How do I live
- Everything I do

www.ingramcontent.com/pod-product-compliance
Lightning Source LLC
Chambersburg PA
CBHW011959090526
44590CB00023B/3789